BIBLICAL PRAYERS
FOR EVERY NEED

by

NORMAN T. SHUERT

Master of Divinity
M.A. in Philosophy, M.A. in Biblical Languages

Copyright © 2011 by Norman Shuert

Biblical Prayers
For Every Need
by Norman Shuert

Printed in the United States of America

ISBN 9781619042421

All rights reserved solely by the author. The author guarantees all contents are original and do not infringe upon the legal rights of any other person or work. No part of this book may be reproduced in any form without the permission of the author. The views expressed in this book are not necessarily those of the publisher.

Unless otherwise indicated, Bible quotations are taken from The New International Version® of the Bible. Copyright © 1973, 1978, 1984 by International Bible Society.

www.xulonpress.com

ACKNOWLEDGEMENTS

The initial draft of this devotional book was used for my private use. It has always been a blessing to me as I have been able to give words to the longings of my heart. I want to thank my family and friends who all asked for copies and encouraged me to share this book with more people by having it printed.

CONTENTS

Forward xiii

Morning Dedication xv

Spiritual Situations

Accepting God's Discipline 19

Afraid 19

Anxious about Promotion, Reputation 20

Choosing Friends 21

Confessing Sin 22

Confident as a Servant of God 23

Confident in God 24

Dedicated to Ministry 26

Depressed 27

Disappointed by a Friend 28

Discouraged 29

Facing Death	29
Facing Enemies	30
Facing Trouble	33
Fighting God's Foes	34
Having Difficulty Accepting Misfortune	38
In a Spiritual Desert	40
Lonely	42
Old	43
Overwhelmed	45
Patient in Suffering	46
Praising God	47
Rejected for being a Christian	49
Rejoicing in God's Coming	50
Rejoicing in God's Deliverance	50
Rejoicing in God's Goodness	51
Rejoicing in God's Victory	52
Repentant	54
Safe in God's Providence	57
Secure in God's care	58
Seeking God	58
Seeking God's Direction	59
Seeking Perspective	61
Seeking Success	63

Sick or Grieving 64
Steadfast in God's Service 66
Tempted To Drink and Party 67
Tempted To Sin 68
Thanking God for Answered Prayer 70
Thanking God for Deliverance 71
Thanking God for Salvation 73
Thirsting for God 74
Trusting God 78
Under Discipline 79
Waiting on God 80
Wanting Justice 81

Petitions

Praying For Character 85
Praying for Contentment 87
Praying for Direction 90
Praying for Fear of the Lord 90
Praying for Generosity 91
Praying for God's Help 92
Praying for Grace to Forgive Others 93
Praying for the Holy Spirit 94
Praying for Hope, Renewal 95

Praying for Joy 96
Praying for Light and Joy 98
Praying for an Obedient Spirit 99
Praying for Peace 100
Praying for Perspective 101
Praying for Protection 102
Praying for Revival 104
Praying for Salvation of the World..................................106
Praying for Strength 108
Praying for Unsaved Friend 109
Praying for Wisdom 110
Praying for World Peace 111

Wonderful Truths

God Controls All..115
God Gives Abundant Life 118
God Gives Salvation 119
God Is Almighty...121
God Is Our Creator 123
God Knows All 124
God Protects His Children 125
God's Presence Is Good 127
God Provides Money..128

God's Word Is Good For Me 129
The Grandeur of God 130
The Lord Alone Is God 131
The Lord Alone Will Be Worshiped 131
The Lord Is My Strength 132
The Lord Provides All My Needs 134
The Lord Rescues His Children 135
Salvation Will Be Victorious 137

Specialized Prayers

Of a Farmer 141
Of a Healed Person 142
Of a Missionary 143
Of a Preacher 145
Of a Retired Person 146
Of a Servant of the Lord 147

These ninety prayers express the spiritual needs and longing of those who earnestly desire to serve God. They are adaptations of passages from the Bible, arranged by topic, and expressed as direct prayers to God.

I often found that when I wanted to use the Bible devotionally to pray for a specific need I was unable to find a passage that spoke directly to my need. So I began compiling these Scripture passages to help me pray in whatever spiritual situation I found myself. I hope they will also assist *you* in praying scripturally and devotionally in *your* life situations.

May the words of my mouth and the meditation of my heart be pleasing in your sight, O Lord, my Rock and my Redeemer. (Psalm 19:14)

Morning Dedication

O Lord God Almighty
    Creator, Master of everything,
        I worship Thee

All I am and have comes from You
    Thank You

Entirely to You,
    I dedicate myself and mine,
        For it is Your due.

From all selfishness, empty me,
    So You may live through me.

May constant praying bring
    Your presence, my strength,
        To make my heart sing.

In me the Spirit and flesh wage war.
    Today, freely may my spirit soar.

My thoughts, words, deeds, and play,
    May they all please You today.

Give self-control to me
    With food, sex, money, tv.

Help me forgive all,
   For every slight, hurt or fall.

Give me peace in every plight,
   O all-providing Father,
     Trusting You to make it right.

Help me bypass the good
   To grasp the best.

Prune my priorities,
   To seek only Your Kingdom,
     In me and humanity.

Fill me with vision and passion
   Till my assignment, Lord is done.

Help me give witness
   Of Jesus Christ, my happiness.

May I intercede,
   For family and friends,
     And all the world in need.

May I give a helping hand,
   Seeing Jesus in every man.

Then surely goodness and mercy,
   Joy and fulfillment
     Will follow me,
        All the days of my life
           Till final ecstasy.

Accepting God's Discipline

O Lord, blessed is the man you discipline and teach from your Word. You grant him relief from days of trouble.

(Psalm 94:12-13)

Afraid

Lord, I'm afraid. I fear what the future may bring. May faith and trust in you wash away my fear. Increase my confidence as I hear you say, "This is what the Lord, your creator, says: 'Fear not, for I have redeemed you. I have called you by name; you are mine. When you pass through the waters, I will be with you. And when you pass through the rivers, they will not sweep over you. When you walk through fire, you will not be burned. Since you are precious and honored in my sight, and because I love you, I will ransom you if you are captured. Do not be afraid, for I am with you.'"

(Isaiah 43:1-5)

Anxious about Promotion, Reputation

No one from the east or the west can exalt a man, but it is God alone who judges. He is the one who brings one down, and exalts another.

(Psalm 75:6-7)

Choosing Friends

O Lord Jesus, my social life is in turmoil. I need your help in picking and making friends. You said that I will be blessed and greatly rewarded if I do not live my life listening to the advice of the ungodly, or loitering in places frequented by sinners, or relaxing and visiting with those who scorn Christianity. But if I delight in your Word and study my Bible daily, I will be like a tree planted by a river that never runs dry, and whose leaves never wither, and which always bears fruit in its proper season. All my endeavors will bear mature fruit. All this happens because you, O Lord, are the Master of all life, and you nurture the life of the Christian dedicated to you.

O Lord, separate me from all my friends and acquaintances who would hinder my devotion to you by their attitudes and advice. Bring me good Christian fellowship. May your saints be the streams of water near which my life is planted and nourished.

(Psalm 1:1-3, 6)

Confessing Sin

O Lord, do not rebuke and discipline me in your anger. Because of my sin, your hand has come down upon me so that there is no health in my body. My guilt has overwhelmed me like a burden too heavy to bear. My sinful folly has left me with loathsome, festering wounds. Bent low, I go about mourning all day long. I am feeble and utterly crushed. My innermost soul groans in anguish. O Lord, you know all my longings, how my heart pounds, my strength fails, my eyes are dull. Even my friends and family avoid me. I am like a deaf man who cannot hear and a mute who cannot speak. O Lord, my pain is always before me. I am about to fall. I am troubled by my sin, and I confess to you my iniquity. Please do not forsake me. Be not far from me. Come quickly to help me, my Lord and my Savior.

(Psalm 38)

Confident as a Servant of God

O Lord, I thank you for being so faithful to me since I dedicated myself to being your servant. It is wonderful to know that you will always be faithful to what you said: "I said, 'You are my servant; I have chosen you and have not rejected you.' So do not fear, for I am with you. Do not be dismayed, for I am your God. I will strengthen you and help you; I will uphold you with my righteous right hand. All who rage against you will surely be ashamed and disgraced. Those who oppose you will be as nothing and perish.

"Though you search for your enemies, you will not find them. Those who wage war against you will be as nothing at all. For I am the Lord, your God, who takes hold of your right hand and says to you, 'Do not fear; I will help you. Do not be afraid, my little one, for I myself will help you,' declares the Lord your redeemer.

I will make rivers flow on barren heights and springs within the valleys. I will turn the desert into pools of water and the parched ground into springs, so that people may see and know that the hand of the Lord has done this."

(Isaiah 41:9-20)

Confident in God

I will praise you, O Lord, with all my heart. I will shout about all your marvelous works. I will be happy and rejoice in you, praising your name, O Most High. For you are a refuge for the oppressed, a fortified castle in times of trouble and desperation. Your people will lean on and confidently trust in you because you have never forsaken those who seek you. The needy will not always be forgotten, nor the hope of the afflicted perish forever, because you are Lord, and your vigilant care is eternal.

(Psalm 9)

Whom should I fear? No one. What should I dread? Nothing, since you, Lord, are my rescue, the stronghold of my life. Though war breaks out and foes attack me, I will remain confident. One thing I ask of you, Lord: that I may dwell in your house all the days of my life, to meditate on your teachings, and to gaze upon your beauty in your sanctuary. For in the day of trouble you will keep me safe in the shelter of your tabernacle. Then I will sing praises to you, Lord, as you rescue me from all my troubles.

Hear my voice, O Lord, and mercifully answer me. My heart tells me to seek your face. I will, because you are the light of my life. Please do not hide your face or turn me away in your anger. You are my savior. Even though my father and mother forsake me, I know you will not forsake me, for you have been my helper in the past. My heart tells me, "Wait for the Lord. Be strong and courageous, and wait for the Lord." With a quiet and confident heart, I will wait for you, Lord, my strength, my shield, my shepherd who carries me.

(Psalm 27; 28:7-9)

Dedicated to Ministry

I am humbled, Lord, that you have called me to do your work. What an awesome privilege it is to be your servant and work in your kingdom to spread the gospel. But it is also scary. Like Isaiah I feel filthy with sin and weakness. He cried, "Woe to me! I am ruined! For I am a man of unclean lips, and I live among a people of unclean lips." But you sent an angel with a burning coal to touch his lips, taking away his guilt and sins. Lord, purify me. Make me pure, holy, and strong. You also want to send me to do your work. I am telling you now, "Here am I. Send me!" Equip me with holiness, wisdom, and strength, so you will be pleased with the fruits of my ministry.

(Isaiah 6:5-8)

Depressed

O Lord, I am pining away and utterly distraught. Do not rebuke me in your anger or discipline me. Be merciful to me for I am faint. All my strength has withered away, all my zest for life has dissipated. Heal me for my bones are in agony. My soul is in anguish. How long, O Lord, how long before you come to heal the hurt that has paralyzed my whole being from within? Turn to me, Lord, and rescue me, not because I deserve it, but because of your unfailing love. I am worn out from groaning; all night long I flood my bed with weeping. My eyes grow weak with sorrow. My body is limp. My spirit is downcast. Lord, save me. Heal me. Return joy and contentment to my heart. Father, teach me to rest in your provision. Teach me to wait for you. But come quickly, Lord, before I despair. You are my only hope

(Psalm 6)

Disappointed by a Friend

If an enemy were insulting me, I could endure it. I could hide from a foe attacking me. But I am reproached by my companion, my close friend with whom I once enjoyed sweet fellowship in the Lord. But I call to you, Lord. I cry out morning, noon, and night. Hear my pleas and rescue me unharmed from the battle waged against me. You say to me, "Cast your cares on me and I will sustain you. I never let the righteous fall." Help me, Lord, to trust in you completely.

(Psalm 55:12-3)

Discouraged

O Lord, my soul is discouraged. It complains, saying: "the path of my life and the causes I work so hard to accomplish are hidden from the Lord. He doesn't care how I am doing."

Lord, let me hear your promises again. Let hope and faith strengthen my soul as I hear you say, "I am the everlasting God who created everything. I will not grow tired or weary. I give strength to the weary. Even though youths sometimes grow tired and weary and young men stumble and fall, those who hope in me will renew their strength. They will soar on wings like eagles. They will run and not grow weary. They will walk and not be faint."

(Isaiah 40:27-31)

Facing Death

I will see your face in righteousness, O Lord. When I awake from death, I will be fully satisfied to find myself beholding your form and having sweet communion with you.

(Psalm 17:15)

Facing Enemies

Vindicate me, O God, and plead my cause against an ungodly nation. Rescue me from deceitful and wicked men. I feel rejected by you, even though you are in fact my stronghold. Why must I go about mourning, oppressed by my enemies? May your truth guide me; may its light make me see and feel your presence. Then I will praise you, O Lord, my joy and my delight. Why are you depressed, O my soul? Why so disturbed within me? Put your hope in God, for I will praise him, my Savior and my God.

(Psalm 43)

Be merciful to me, O God, for men hotly pursue me. They boldly press their attack against me all day long. But when I am afraid, I will trust in you, whose word I praise and trust. Of course I will not be afraid, for what can mortal men do to me? All day long they twist my words and plot to harm me. They observe all my movements hoping for an opportunity to kill me. O Lord, keep a record of my tears and lament. In you I trust and I will not be afraid, because my enemies will turn back when I call on you. This will prove that you are for me. What can man do to me since you are my protector? I will praise and thank you for you have kept me from stumbling. You have delivered me from death, so that I may walk before you in the light of life.

Psalm 56

Please, O Lord my God, have mercy on me. I am faced with disaster, but I will take refuge in the shadow of your wings until it has passed. I will cry out to you, O Most High, because you never fail to fulfill your purposes for me. From heaven you reach out with love and faithfulness and save me from those who hotly pursue me. I am in the midst of men who are like ravenous beasts—whose teeth are spears and arrows and whose tongues are sharp swords. I've been scared because they laid a trap for me, but they themselves have fallen into it. O my Savior, my heart is steadfast. Awake, O my soul, and sing and make music. Exalt the Lord in heaven. May his glory be over all the earth. I will praise you, Lord, among the nations, for great is your love, and your faithfulness reaches to the skies. Be exalted, O God, above the heavens, and let your glory be over all the earth.

(Psalm 57)

Give us aid against the enemy, O Lord, for the help of man is worthless. You will trample down our enemies. With you, O God, we will gain the victory.

(Psalm 60:11-12)

Facing Trouble

Listen to my prayer, O God. Do not ignore my plea, but give me a quick answer. My thoughts trouble me. I am distraught by the stares of the wicked and the voice of the enemy. These cause me to suffer greatly. My heart is full of anguish and I am overwhelmed with fear and trembling as the terrors and horror of death attack me. My weak spirit longs to escape all this and says to me, "Oh, I wish I had the wings of a dove! I would fly away and be at rest. I would fly very far away and stay in some deserted place where I would be safe from this tempest and storm." But I call to you, Lord, I cry out morning, noon, and night. You hear my pleas and rescue me unharmed from the battle waged against me. You say to me, "Cast your cares on me and I will sustain you. I never let the righteous fall." Help me, Lord, to trust in you completely.

(Psalm 55:12-23)

Fighting God's Foes

Lord, your servant gets so dejected and discouraged as I battle to spread your gospel. There are so many obstacles, so many people who hinder the spread of your kingdom. So many rise up against me. By faith I know you are a shield around me. You are my glory who lifts up my head. To you, O Lord, I cry, "help!" Lift up my head. Encourage my heart lest I faint in doing your work. I will face another day because I know you will sustain me. Deliver me from all my enemies. I will not fear because deliverance comes from you Lord. May your blessing be on your people. O my soul, rest in your Lord, for his mercy endures forever.

(Psalm 3)

Arise, O Lord, let not man triumph; let the nations be judged in your presence. Put them in fear; let the nations know that they are but men. May they recognize you, and fear you, their maker and king. They should, because the earth is yours, and everything and everybody in it. You created the earth, the sky, the oceans, the whole universe. May the nations allow your church the freedom to thrive.

(Psalm 9:19-20; 24:1-2)

Why do you stand far off, O Lord? Why do you hide yourself in times of trouble? But I know that you are King forever and ever. The nations will perish before you. I know you hear the desire of the afflicted. You encourage them and listen to their cry, defending the fatherless and the oppressed, so that worldly men will no longer terrify your people.

(Psalm 10:1,16-18)

Deliver me from my enemies, O God. Protect me from evildoers who conspire against me, even though I've done them no wrong. They are ready to attack me though I've caused no offense. Look on my plight and arise to help me, O Lord God Almighty. As Head of your church, rouse yourself to punish all the nations, showing no mercy to these wicked traitors. You scoff at all the nations who proudly prowl the city like snarling dogs, spewing swords from their lips, and thinking no one will control them or punish them. O God, my loving Lord, I am waiting upon you to be my strength and my fortress. You will go before me and will let me gloat over those who slander me. Let them be caught in their pride for all their curses and lies. May your wrath consume them until they are no more. Then it will be known to the ends of the earth that God rules over his people. Though they continue to live wickedly, I will sing of your strength. In the morning I will sing of your love, for you are my refuge in times of trouble.

I sing praises to you, my loving God, my strength, my safe haven of protection.

(Psalm 59)

O God, do not keep silent. Arise. See how your enemies are astir, how your foes rear their heads. With cunning they conspire against your church and plot against those you cherish. "Come," they say, "let us destroy them so that the name of Jesus Christ will be remembered no more." Make them like tumbleweed, O my God, like chaff before the wind. Terrify them with your might as a raging forest fire sets the mountains ablaze. Cover their faces with shame so that men will seek you, O Lord. May they ever be ashamed and dismayed. May they perish in disgrace. Let them know that you, whose name is the Lord, that you alone are the Most High over all the earth.

(Psalm 83)

O Lord my God, you are my strength and refuge. You are always there when I need help. Therefore I will not be afraid even if earthquakes crumble buildings and mountains fall into the sea. You dwell within your church, so she will not fall.

Nations are in an uproar and kingdoms fall, and even the earth melts when you speak. You make wars cease all over the world. You destroy the weapons of war. You say to me, "Be still and know that I am God; I will be exalted among the nations." O Lord God Almighty, you are indeed with me. You are my fortress.

(Psalm 46)

You foil the plans of all nations and thwart their purposes. But your plans stand firm forever and your heart's purposes last through all generations.

(Psalm 33:10-11)

Let me stand boldly and defiantly shout in the face of the enemy, "Prepare for battle, and be shattered! Devise your strategy, but it will be thwarted; propose your plan, but it will not stand, for God is with us." I will not fear the enemy, for you are the Lord God Almighty. You alone are holy and no one should be feared except you.

(Isaiah 8:9-13)

Having Difficulty Accepting Misfortune

How long, O Lord, must I call for help, but you do not listen? How long must I cry out to you to rescue me from all the violence, injustice and destruction that surrounds me? But you do not save me. Everywhere there is strife and conflict. The law is paralyzed. Justice never prevails. The wicked pervert justice to take advantage of the righteous. How long must I suffer before you do something to rescue me?

You answer me, "Look and watch and be utterly amazed. For I am going to do something in your days that you would not believe even if you were told."

(Habakkuk 1:2-5)

O Lord, are you not from everlasting? My God, my Holy One, your eyes are too pure to look on evil. You cannot tolerate wrong. Why are you silent while the wicked swallow up the righteous? I will stand, like a sentry on guard duty, and I will look to see what answer you will give to my complaint. You answer me:"Write down the revelation plainly on a poster so that it can be read by all as a herald runs with it. For the revelation awaits an appointed time. It will not prove false. Though it lingers, wait for it. It will certainly come and will not delay. The righteous must live by faith in my faithfulness."

(Habakkuk 1:12-13, 2:1-4)

Lord, give me the faith of Habakkuk, so I can say with him: I heard and my heart pounded, my lips quivered at the sound; decay crept into my bones, and my legs trembled. Yet I will wait patiently for the day of calamity. Though the fig tree does not bud and there are no grapes on the vines, though the olive crop fails and the fields produce no food, though there are no sheep in the pen and no cattle in the stalls, yet I will rejoice in the Lord. I will be joyful in God my Savior. The Sovereign Lord is my strength. He makes my feet like the feet of a deer, enabling me to go on the rocky heights without falling.

(Habakkuk 3:16-19)

In a Spiritual Desert

I have been crying out to you for help, O God. I've been in great distress. I have sought you at night with untiring outstretched hands, but my soul refuses to be comforted. My spirit has grown faint and I've been too troubled to speak or sleep. I am overwhelmed. I thought about former days when my heart enjoyed sweet meditations. I remembered my songs in the night in your presence. But now I ask, "Will you reject forever? Will you never show your favor again? Has your unfailing love vanished forever? Has your promise failed for all time? Have you forgotten to be merciful? Are you angry with me, and therefore have withheld your compassion?" Woe is me, because your right hand deals differently with me now. Gone are the days of sweet communion in your presence.

However, from this spiritual desert I will remember your deeds, O Lord God Almighty. Yes, I will remember your miracles and wonderful deeds throughout my life. I will meditate on all your good works. Your ways, O God, are always holy. What god is as great as my God? You are the God who performs miracles. You have displayed your power throughout the world. With your mighty arm you have redeemed your people. Lord, come quickly and rescue me from perishing in this desert. I need your mercy. I need the touch of your presence to sustain me. Come Lord Jesus. Come quickly.

(Psalm 77:1-15)

Lonely

O God, you have promised to be a father to the fatherless and a defender of widows. Please, be my father and provider. You said you would set prisoners free and set the lonely in families. O Lord, rescue me from my loneliness and make my heart sing for the joy of having the love of family and friends.

(Psalm 68:5-6)

O Jesus, turn to me and be gracious to me, for I am lonely and afflicted. I am overcome by the many troubles in my heart. Please free me from my anguish. Look upon my affliction and my distress and take away all my sins. I am hoping in you to give me refuge and protection. Safeguard my life. Let me not fall in shame. May integrity and righteous living protect me. Rescue me, O Lord, from all my troubles. You are my only hope.

(Psalm 25:16-22)

Old

O Lord, I have taken refuge in you. Rescue and deliver me in your righteousness. Turn your ear to me and never let me be put to shame. Be my rock of refuge to which I can always go. Deliver me from the hand of the wicked, from the grasp of cruel men. O Sovereign Lord, I will praise you forever since you brought me forth from my mother's womb. You have been my confidence since my youth. Even from birth I have relied on you. I declare your splendor all day long.

Do not cast me away when I am old and my strength is gone. Do not forsake me when I am old and gray until I declare your power to the next generations. O Lord, you have done great things. Your righteousness reaches to the skies. Who is like you? Though you have made me see many bitter troubles, you will restore my life again. You will increase my honor and comfort me once again. I will praise you for your faithfulness, O God. I will shout for joy and sing praises to you. My tongue will tell of your righteous acts all day long, for you have redeemed me. You have put to shame and confusion those who wanted to harm me.

(Psalm 71)

O Lord, my God who rescues me, I cry out to you both day and night. Please hear my prayer, for my soul is full of trouble and my life draws near the grave. I am counted among those who are about to die. I have no strength, like a dead man lying in a coffin. You have put me in the lowest pit, in the darkest depths. Your wrath lies heavily upon me. You have taken from me my closest friends and have made me repulsive to them. I am confined and cannot escape. My eyes are dim with grief. Everyday I raise my hands and call out to you, O Lord. In the morning my prayer for help comes before you. Why, O God, do you reject me and hide your face from me? O Lord, bless me with your presence. Come quickly to rescue me, for you have taken my companions and loved ones from me. Darkness is my closest friend.

(Psalm 88)

Overwhelmed

O Lord, I come to you crushed and desperate. I am so overwhelmed by the burdens of my life. I can't take it any more. The words of Moses so accurately express my desperately hopeless situation: "Why have you brought this trouble on your servant? What have I done to displease you that you put the burden of all these people on me? Did I conceive all these people? Did I give them birth? Why do you tell me to carry them in my arms, as a nurse carries an infant? I cannot carry all these people by myself; the burden is too heavy for me. If this is how you are going to treat me, put me to death right now." (Numbers 11:11-15)

You answered Moses, "Is the Lord's arm too short? You will see whether or not what I say will come true for you" (Numbers 11:23). Hear my desperate cry as you heard his. You answered his prayer by giving him 70 assistants. Please Lord, give me some assistance so that I will not break under this load of responsibility that is too heavy for me to carry alone. Come quickly, Lord, to help me. Come quickly. And as I wait for your deliverance, give me the faith to trust that your arm is truly not too short.

Patient in Suffering

O Lord, use Job to teach me to be patient in my sufferings. Create in me the same spirit that was in Job when he said, "The Lord gave and the Lord has taken away; may the name of the Lord be praised." He also said, "Shall we accept good from God and not trouble?" Create in me that absolute faith and trust in you who sovereignly controls all things for our good. You indeed make all things beautiful in its time.

(Job 1:21, 2:10; Ecclesiastes 3:11)

Praising God

We sing to you, O Lord, a new song. With all the earth we praise your name, proclaiming your salvation day after day. We declare your glory around the world for your marvelous deeds among all peoples. For you are great, Lord, and most worthy of praise, to be feared above all gods. All the gods of the nations are idols, but you made the heavens. Splendor and majesty are before you, strength and glory are in your sanctuary.

May all the nations give you the glory due your name. May all the earth tremble before you and worship you in the splendor of your holiness. We proclaim throughout the world, that you reign as Lord over all. The world is firmly established and cannot be moved, and you will come and judge all peoples with justice. Oh, may the whole world rejoice with us. Let the heavens rejoice and the earth be glad. Let the sea resound and all that is in it. Let the fields be jubilant and all the trees of the forest sing for joy. For you, our Lord and Master, is coming to judge the earth and you will judge the world and all its people in righteousness and truth.

(Psalm 96)

O Lord, you are my God. I will exalt you and praise your name, for in perfect faithfulness you have done marvelous things that you planned long ago. You have been a refuge for the poor and for the needy in distress, a shelter from the storms of life and a shade from the heat. I also praise you in advance for what you will do. You will destroy the shroud that covers all nations and you will swallow up death forever. You will wipe away the tears from all faces and remove the disgrace of your people from all the earth. Surely you are our God. We trust you. We rejoice in your salvation.

(Isaiah 25:1-9)

Biblical Prayers

Rejected for being a Christian

Save me, O God, for the waters have come up to my neck, and I am sinking because there is no foothold in the miry depths. My eyes are red, my throat parched, and I am worn out calling to you for help. Those who hate me without reason outnumber the hairs of my head. I endure scorn and shame for your sake. I am even rejected by my family, so that I've become a stranger to my brothers. Why? Because the zeal of your house consumes me and the insults aimed at you, Lord, fall on me.

In your great love, O God, answer me with your sure salvation. Rescue me from the mire. Don't let the floodwaters of rejection engulf me and swallow me up. In your great mercy turn to me. Do not hide from your servant. Come quickly for I am in great trouble. Redeem me from my foes. Scorn has broken my heart and left me helpless. I looked for sympathy, but there was none. I found no comforters. In my pain and distress, protect me. I will praise your name, O Lord, in song and glorify you with thanksgiving. I will take courage because I know you are the God who hears his needy servants. Come quickly. Give me more faith and patience as I wait for my rescue by your hand.

(Psalm 69)

Rejoicing in God's Coming

My heart is glad, O Lord, because you proclaim comfort to your people. You speak tenderly to us, telling us our sins have been paid for with more than enough payment. And every valley will be raised up, and every hill made low, and the rough ground leveled so that you can come swiftly on a super highway. Your glory will be revealed to us and to all mankind. Alleluia!

(Isaiah 40:1-5)

Rejoicing in God's Deliverance

I will bless you, Lord, at all times. Your praise will always be on my lips. I will brag about your goodness. All you who are afflicted, listen to my report: I sought the Lord, and he answered me. He delivered me from all my fears. So rejoice with me and join me in glorifying and praising the Lord.

(Psalm 34:1-4)

Rejoicing in God's Goodness

O Lord, may all the earth come before you with joyful songs, worshiping you with gladness and shouting for joy. We know that you, Lord, are God. It is you who made us and we are your people and the sheep of your pasture. Let us enter your gates with thanksgiving and your courts with praise, giving thanks to you. For you are good and your love endures forever. Your faithfulness continues through all generations.

(Psalm 100)

O Lord, you are my God and I earnestly seek you. My soul thirsts for you and my body longs for you in a dry and weary land with no water. I have seen your power and glory in church. My lips will glorify you because your love is better than life. I will praise you as long as I live, and in your name I will lift up my hands. My soul will be satisfied as with the richest of foods. I meditate on your goodness through the night. I sing in the shadow of your wings because you are helping me, and my soul clings to you because your right hand is upholding me.

(Psalm 63:1-8)

Rejoicing in God's Victory

O Lord, I rejoice in your strength. How great is my joy in your salvation, in the victories you continually give! You have given me the desires of my heart and have not withheld the requests of my prayers. You blessed me with rich blessings and placed a crown of glory on my head. I asked for life and you have given me length of days, forever and ever. My glory is great through your victories. Surely you have made me exceedingly glad with the joy of your presence, and granted me eternal blessings. I trust and rely on you. Through your mercy and unfailing love, O Most High God, I will never be shaken.

(Psalm 21:1-7)

I am like an olive tree flourishing in your house. I trust in your unfailing love forever and ever. I will praise you forever in the presence of your saints for what you have done. All my hope I place in your name, which is so good.

(Psalm 52:8-9)

You are our king and God who decrees victories for your church. Through you we push back our enemies and trample our foes. We do not trust in guns or armies to bring us victory. No, it is you who gives us victory over our enemies.

(Psalm 44:4-7)

I surely know that you are my help. You are my Lord who sustains me. I will make an extra contribution to the spread of your kingdom to express my gratitude. I will testify of your goodness, for you have delivered me from all my troubles, and my eyes have looked in triumph on my foes.

(Psalm 54:4-7)

Repentant

O God my Father, with tears and deep helpless sorrow I come humbly before you. Please have mercy on me. Blot out my transgressions because of your unfailing love and great compassion. Cleanse me from my sin and wash away the wickedness in my soul. I know my sin so very well; it is always before me. I cannot forget it even for a moment.

I have done evil in your sight. Though others may be hurt by my sin, my sin is really against you. I have offended you. You are absolutely right and just when you judge me. I do deserve your anger and punishment. I was born with a sinful nature and I have sinned ever since my birth. But you don't want this. You want truth and wisdom within my soul. Teach me, train me, Jesus.

Only if you cleanse me, will I be clean. If you wash me, then I will be whiter than snow. Then my bones will dance in merriment, and my crushed spirit rejoice with great gladness. Hide your face from my sins and blot out all my iniquity.

Create in me a pure heart, O God, and renew a steadfast spirit within me. Do not cast me from your presence or take your Holy Spirit from me. Restore to me the joy of your salvation and willing spirit, to sustain me. Only then will I be able to work for you and minister to your people. Only then will I be able to teach unbelievers your ways and turn sinners back to you.

(Psalm 51)

When I did not confess my sin to you, my body ached from the groaning of my downcast spirit. Both day and night your hand was heavy upon me, convicting me of my shame. My strength was sapped as in the heat of summer. But when I acknowledged my sin and openly confessed it to you, then you forgave my sin and washed away my guilt and shame. Oh! What a wonderful savior you are! May everyone pray and find you as I have, and have their sins washed away. You are my hiding place. You will protect me from trouble and fill my heart with songs of deliverance.

(Psalm 32:1-7)

Say to me, Lord, "Though your sins are like scarlet, they shall be as white as snow; though they are red as crimson, they shall be like wool. If you are willing and obedient, you will eat the best from the land." O Lord, help me to be willing and obedient.

(Isaiah 1:18-19)

O Lord, give me the forgiveness you promised when you said, "I, even I, am he who blots out your transgressions, for my own sake, and remembers your sins no more."

(Isaiah 43:25)

"Remember that you are my servant and I will never forget you. I have swept away your offenses like a cloud, your sins like the morning mist. Return to me for I have already redeemed you."

(Isaiah 44:21-22)

How fortunate and blessed am I, because my transgressions are forgiven, and my sins covered so that you do not see them, O Lord. You do not count my sin against me. Praise your name.

Safe in God's Providence

Continue to keep me in the safety of Your protection, O Lord. I confess that apart from You I have nothing that is good. But with you I have everything that is good. You have assigned me my provisions of food, clothing, and shelter, and made my good fortune secure. My home is in a pleasant place. My heritage and my inheritance are beautiful to me. I praise you, Lord, for counseling me and instructing my heart every night. I fix my gaze upon you. I will never be shaken because you are at my right hand. My heart is glad, my tongue rejoices, and my body rests secure, because you will not even abandon me at the grave. You have made known to me the path to life after the grave. I will be filled with the joy of your presence at your right hand. I will enjoy eternal pleasures. Alleluia! Thank you, Jesus, for eternal life. You, O Lord, are my inheritance, and in your presence is fullness of joy.

(Psalm 16)

Secure in God's care

How secure I feel in your care, O Lord! You are the Sovereign Master with absolute power over all existing things. You tend your flock like a shepherd, gathering the lambs in your arms and carrying them close to your heart. You gently lead those who move slower because they have young ones. Your reward is always with you. O how good it is to be one in your flock!

(Isaiah 40:10-11)

Seeking God

O Lord my God, my heart has grown cold. Please inflame my heart by your Holy Spirit, so that I will hunger and thirst after you. You have promised that if I seek you, my Lord and God, I will find him if I look for you with all my heart and with all my soul. This is what I want to do. Create this desire in me and purify me from any obstacles to this kind of devotion.

(Deut. 4:29)

Seeking God's Direction

In you, O Lord my God, I entrust my soul. As long as I put my trust in You, I will never be ashamed. Lord, never let me be put to shame. Show me Your ways, guide me in Your truth, for You are my Savior, and in You alone is my hope for the future. Do not remember the sins and rebellion of my youth, but remember Your eternal mercy and great love. Act according to Your goodness and love, and not as my sins deserve.

You are good and upright, O Lord. That's why you instruct your children in your ways. You guide the humble in the right way to live. All who obey enjoy the fruit of your loving faithfulness. You instruct them in the way you have chosen for them. You even confide in them, revealing your gospel to them. My eyes are always on you, O Lord, for only you will release my feet from the snare.

(Psalm 25:1-15)

You said, "I will instruct you and teach you in the way you should go; I will give you counsel and watch over you. But do not be stubborn and require that I control you with a bit and bridle, like a mule." I know that if I go my own way, I will encounter many woes. But if I trust in you, Lord, your unfailing love will continuously surround me. Please make me sensitive to your quiet voice so that a painful bit is not needed to guide me according to your will.

(Psalm 32:8-10)

How gracious you are, O Lord my God, when I cry for help. As soon as you hear, you answer me. And though I feed on adversity and affliction, your teaching will be hidden no more. You promised that whether I turn to the right or to the left, my ears will hear a voice behind me saying, "This is the way; walk in it." O Lord, may this be so in my life. Come quickly Lord as I wait upon you.

(Isaiah 30:19-21)

Seeking Perspective

Surely you are good to your church, O God, to those who are pure of heart. But at times I have slipped nearly losing my foothold, because I envied the prosperity of the wicked. They seem to be healthy and strong, without struggles and free from the burdens most men have. In their arrogance they threaten to oppress others. They claim to possess the earth; they even lay claim to heaven. It seems they are carefree and their wealth always increasing. These thoughts have plagued me all day long. I thought to myself that I have kept my heart pure and innocent all in vain. My heart was grieved and my spirit bitter. I was like an ignorant brute beast before you.

When I tried to understand all this, it was oppressive to me until I entered your sanctuary, O Lord, then I understood their final destiny. Surely you place them on slippery ground that ends in ruin. How suddenly are they destroyed and completely swept away by terrors! When you arise, O Lord, you will despise them as fantasies.

The truth of the matter is that you are always with me; you are holding me by my right hand. You guide me with your advice and afterward you will take me into glory. Whom have I in heaven except you? And the earth has nothing I desire except you. My flesh and heart may fail, but you are the strength of my heart and my portion forever. In the end, O Sovereign Lord, you will destroy all who are unfaithful to you. All who are far from you will surely perish. But as for me, it is good to be near you, my God and Father. I have made you my refuge. I will tell people of all your deeds.

(Psalm 73)

Seeking Success

Help me, O God, to take to heart your instruction on how to be successful, saying: "Be careful to obey all the law my servants gave you; do not turn from it to the right or to the left, that you may be successful wherever you go. Do not let the Bible depart from your mouth; meditate on it day and night, so that you may be careful to do everything written in it. Then you will be prosperous and successful."

(Joshua 1:7-9)

Sick or Grieving

Be merciful to me, O Lord, for I am in distress; my eyes grow weak with sorrow, my soul and my body are weak with grief. My life is consumed by anguish and my years by groaning; my strength fails because of my affliction, and my bones grow weak. I will be glad and rejoice in your love, however, for you see my affliction and know the anguish of my soul. You have not let the enemy triumph over me, but you have made me sure-footed on a flat and wide path.

In you, O Lord, I have taken refuge; deliver me in your righteousness. Turn your ear to me, and quickly come to my rescue. For the sake of your name lead and guide me. Free me from any trap the devil sets for me. Into your hands I commit my spirit; save me, O Lord God. I trust you. I say to myself, "You are my God." My times are in your hands. Let your face shine on your servant; save me in your unfailing love and mercy. Let me never be put to shame, because I have trusted in your protection. Hide me in the shelter of your presence from the intrigues of this world and from the accusing tongues of men.

Praise be to you, O Lord, for you showed your wonderful love to me when I was besieged with trouble. In my alarm I thought I was cut off from your sight. Yet you heard my cry for mercy when I called to you for help. May all your saints love you Lord, because you preserve the faithful. May they all be strong and courageous. May I be strong and courageous.

(Psalm 31)

Lord, you promised that if I cared for the weak, you would deliver me in times of trouble, that you would protect me and preserve my life, that you would sustain me on my sickbed and restore me from my hospital bed. I now pray, Lord, have mercy on me. Heal me even though I have sinned against you. Raise me up. I know I am your child. Uphold me. May I feel and enjoy your presence forever.

(Psalm 41)

Steadfast in God's Service

O Sovereign Lord, you have instructed my tongue to know the word that sustains the weary. You have opened my ears and I have not been rebellious. I have not drawn back from obeying you. Because you help me, I will not be disgraced. Therefore, I have set my face like flint and I know I will not be put to shame. He who vindicates me is near, so who is there to accuse or condemn me? They will all wear out like a garment and be eaten by moths.

(Isaiah 50:4-9)

Tempted To Drink and Party

O Lord, teach me your ways and train me to live my life according to your instructions. You have said, "Woe to those who are heroes at drinking wine and champions at mixing drinks. Woe to those who rise early in the morning to run after their drinks and who stay up late at night till they are inflamed with beer and wine. They party with live bands and much drinking, having no respect for their bodies which are your creation and no regard for your instruction. Therefore they will be exiled from my kingdom for lack of understanding." O Lord, rescue me from drunkenness and wild partying. Help me to live a sober and serious life dedicated to pleasing you and doing your work.

(Isaiah 5:22, 11-13)

Tempted To Sin

O Lord, help me. I am being tempted to sin against you and I desperately need your help. I'm so weak and I will fall without your help. I know that your commands are not too difficult for me or beyond my reach. As you said through Moses, "It is not up in heaven, so that you have to ask, 'Who will cross the seas to get it and proclaim it to us so we may obey it?' No, the word is very near you; it is in your mouth and in your heart so you may obey it."

Satan lies to me as he did to Eve, telling me, "this sin is not really sin. In this situation it is okay, or at least it is not that bad and God will readily forgive you." But you speak to your people very clearly: "See, I set before you today life and prosperity, death and destruction. For I command you today to love the Lord your God, to walk in his ways, and to keep his commands; then you will live and increase, and the Lord your God will bless you. But if your heart turns away and you are not obedient, I declare to you this day that you will certainly be destroyed. I have set before you life and death, blessings and curses. Now choose life, so that you and your children may live and that you may love the Lord your God. Listen to his voice, and hold fast to him, for the Lord is your life." O Lord, give me the strength to choose life by loving and obeying you. Let not Satan or my flesh rule over me.

(Deut. 30:11-20)

You tell me, "Be strong and courageous. Do not be afraid or discouraged, for I, the Lord your God, go with you; I will never leave you nor forsake you." Lord, help me put my trust in you. Be my strength. Deliver me from temptation and evil. Don't leave me now.

(Deut. 31:6)

Thanking God for Answered Prayer

Come and listen, all you who fear God. Let me tell you what he has done for me when I cried out to him for help. If I had cherished sin in my heart, the Lord would not have listened, but God has surely listened and heard my prayers. Praise the Lord with me, who has not rejected my prayer or withheld his love for me!

(Psalm 66:16-20)

Thanking God for Deliverance

I will exalt you, O Lord, for you lifted me out of the depths of my troubles. They did not drown me because I called to you for help, and you healed me. You spared me, snatching me from the grave I was about to lie in. Praise the Lord with me, all my Christian friends. For his anger lasts only for a moment. His favor, however, lasts for a lifetime. Weeping may remain for a night, but a shout of joy comes in the morning. O Lord, you turned my wailing into dancing, my frown into laughter, my depression into joy, so that I would sing your praises. I will give you thanks forever. You are indeed my Savior.

(Psalm 30)

O Lord, you are my rock, my fortress, my shield, and my deliverer. You save me from violent men. Destruction overwhelmed me, the wave of death swirled about me and the cords of the grave coiled around me. In my distress I called out to you for help, and you heard my prayer. You reached down from heaven and took hold of me. You rescued me from my foes, who were too strong for me.

You rescued me because you delight in me.

To the faithful you show yourself faithful. To the blameless you show yourself blameless. To the pure you show yourself pure. You save the humble. You are my lamp, O Lord, turning my darkness into light. With your help I can advance against a whole troop. With your help no wall is too high to scale. Your ways, O God, are perfect and flawless. You arm me with strength and make my way perfect. You make my feet like the feet of mountain deer, enabling me to stand surefooted on the narrow mountain trails. You widen the path for me so I don't twist my ankle. You give me your shield of victory, and you stoop down to make me great.

(2 Samuel 22)

Thanking God for Salvation

O Lord, I will praise you. Although you were angry with me, you turned your anger away and have comforted me. You indeed are my salvation. I will trust and not be afraid because you are my strength and my song. With joy I have drawn water from the wells of salvation. O fellow Christians, may we all give thanks to the Lord and call upon his name. May we make what he has done known among the nations and proclaim that his name should be exalted. Let's sing to the Lord for he has done glorious things and let's make this known to all the world. Shout aloud and sing for joy, O Church, for great is the Lord amongst us!

(Isaiah 12:1-6)

Thirsting for God

My soul thirsts for you, O God. As the deer pants for streams of water, so my soul pants for you. When can I come and meet with the living God? My tears have been my food both day and night while the enemy taunts me, "Where is your God?"

I say, "O God, my rock, Why have you forgotten me? Why must I go about mourning, oppressed by my flesh?" My soul suffers mortal agony as the enemy taunts me, "Where is your strength? Where is your deliverer?" Why are you so downcast, O my soul? Why so disturbed within me? Though I am weak and fail, will God's mercy fail? Will his forgiveness cease? Is the Lord blind? Is his arm too short to help me?

(Psalm 42)

Lord, you are my God, earnestly I seek you. My soul thirsts for you, my body longs for you in an arid place. My heart and my flesh cry out for the living God. My soul faints to feel your presence.

(Psalms 63:1, 84:1-2)

O Lord, hear my prayer, listen to my cry for mercy; in your faithfulness and righteousness, come to my relief. Do not bring your servant into judgment, for no one living is righteous before you. The enemy pursues me, he crushes me to the ground; he makes me dwell in darkness. So my spirit grows faint within me; my heart is dismayed. I spread out my hands to you; my soul is in a parched land and thirsts for you. Answer me quickly, O Lord; my spirit faints with longing. Do not hide your face from me lest I perish. My flesh rebels against me; rescue me. For your name's sake, O Lord, preserve my life; in your righteousness, bring me out of trouble. In your unfailing love, silence my enemies; destroy all my foes, for I am your servant. Be my strength.

(Psalm 14)

Your word gives light; it gives understanding to the simple. I will obey your word. Turn to me and have mercy on me, as you always do to those who love you. Direct my footsteps according to your word; let no sin rule over me. Redeem me from the oppression of my flesh, that I may obey your commands. Streams of tears flow from my eyes, for I fail to obey your word. Make your face shine upon your servant.

(Psalm 119:129-136)

As I pour out my soul, I remember your sweet presence in days gone by. I remember your presence in corporate worship, in all night prayer vigils, in fasting, in studies and meditations. I have felt your presence and seen your power work through me to minister to your children. I have seen your miracles, your power and glory. How sweet is your presence! Your love is better than life. May I sing in the shadow of your wings. May my soul cling to you; may your right hand uphold me. Then I will be satisfied as with the richest of foods, then with singing lips my mouth will praise you. Blessed are those who dwell in your presence. Blessed are those whose strength is in you as they make their pilgrimage through life. They go from strength to strength, till they appear before your throne.

Seek the Lord while he may be found; call on him while he is near. Let the wicked forsake his way and the evil man his thoughts. Let him turn to the Lord, and he will have mercy on him. Let him turn to our God, for he will freely pardon.

Listen to the Lord as he calls, "Come, all you who are thirsty, come to the waters. You who have no money, come, buy and eat!

Come, buy food without money. Why spend money on what is not bread, and your labor on what does not satisfy? Listen, listen to me, and eat what is good, and your soul will delight in the richest of fare. Give ear and come to me; hear me, that your soul may live. I will make an everlasting covenant with you, promising my faithful love forever."

(Isaiah 55:1-31)

Listen to Jesus as he calls: "If anyone is thirsty, let him come to me and drink. Whoever believes in me, streams of living water—my Spirit—will flow from within him. I am the Alpha and the Omega, the Beginning and the End. To him who is thirsty I will give to drink without cost from the spring of the water of eternal life. He who overcomes will inherit all this, and I will be his God and he will be my son. He will sit next to me on my throne.

(Matthew 11:28-30, John 7:37-38, Revelation 21:6-7)

Blessed are those who hunger and thirst for righteousness within themselves, for they will be filled with satisfaction. Lord, come to me in your power, that I may be able to love you with all my heart, and with all my soul, and with all my mind, and with all my strength.

(Matthew 5:6, Mark 12:30)

Trusting God

O God, who always does right, I need you. Answer me when I call; give me relief from my distress. Be full of mercy toward me; hear my plea. How long must I be surrounded by men who love delusions and seek false gods? They are deceived and chase after empty dreams. In my stress I will not sin, but I will search my heart and silently wait on you, for I know that you have set me apart for yourself and hear my prayers. I will trust in you. Let the light of your face shine upon me, O Lord. You have been faithful and have filled my heart with greater joy than great profits from business, or a bountiful harvest, or winning a lottery. I will sleep in peace because you alone, O Lord, make me dwell in safety. My future is secure in your hands.

(Psalm 4)

Under Discipline

I know that you, Lord, discipline me just as I discipline my children. I know you send difficulties to humble me and to test me in order to know what is in my heart, whether or not I would keep your commands.

(Deut. 8:2-5)

Waiting on God

O Lord, teach me to wait quietly for you. You have said, "In repentance and rest is your salvation. In quietness and trust is your strength." How wonderful it is that you long to be gracious to me and rise up to show compassion to me. You indeed are a God of justice. Blessed are all who wait for you!

(Isaiah 30:15,18)

Wanting Justice

What a wicked world we live in! The politicians speak with evasive double-talk and lies. The courts so often let the criminals go without just punishment. There is so much social and racial injustice. Violence is rampant in our cities. The wicked are like cobras with venom of corruption and destruction. Lord, break their fangs. Tear out the teeth of these lions. May the wicked vanish like the water, which quickly runs off after a rain. May the wicked disappear like the slug melting away as it moves along, leaving its trail of slime. Lord, hasten your judgment day when the wicked will surely be swept away. Then the righteous will be glad when they are avenged. Then we will say, "Surely the righteous are still rewarded; surely there is a God who judges the earth." Lord, come quickly and judge the wickedness that abounds all around me.

(Psalm 58)

Praying For Character

O Lord, I want to dwell in the sanctuary of your presence. But who can do this? Only he whose life-style is blameless, who always does what is right, who speaks the truth from his heart, who does not slander or cut down his fellow man, who also keeps his word as an oath, and does not hurt or take advantage of anyone. Such a man will never be shaken.

(Psalm 15)

Who may enter the sanctuary of the Lord? Who may stand in his holy place, commune with him and enjoy his presence? He who has clean hands, a pure heart, a truthful tongue, and whose heart does not pursue worthless things.

(Psalm 24:3-4)

Lord, I want to be like this, so I can walk in your presence without shame. Help me to be more and more like this, for your honor.

Lord, keep my heart pure, solely devoted to you. Don't let me ever be counted among the people who come near to you with their mouth and honor you with their lips, but their hearts are far from you, who worship you according to man made rules. Help me never get my perspective turned upside down, switching the role of potter and clay. Shall what is formed say to him who formed it, "He did not make me?" Can the pot say of the potter, "He knows nothing?" May I always honor and serve you as my creator and master. May I always be your humble and faithful servant.

(Isaiah 29:13-16)

O Lord, may the Spirit of the Lord rest upon me, as Jesus lives within me and I grow more and more like him, just as it did upon him — a Spirit of wisdom and of understanding, the Spirit of counsel and of power, the Spirit of knowledge and of the fear of the Lord. May I delight in the fear of you, Lord. May righteousness be my belt and faithfulness the sash around my waist.

(Isaiah 11:2-5)

Praying for Contentment

Lord, you said to Abraham, "Do not be afraid, I am your shield, your very great reward." Please be my shield. Protect me from the attacks of the devil and the temptations of my flesh. And as you provide me safe passage through life, may I seek only you as my reward. May I be content no matter what works I accomplish, no matter what fruits of my ministry I see, no matter what success I can measure. May I be happy and content just knowing that I am your bride and that you love me more than I can comprehend. Can there be any greater reward, any greater joy or blessing than your love and knowing I will be in your love forever? May my soul rest in peace and great joy despite any circumstances, because you, and only you, are my very great reward.

(Gen. 15:1)

O Lord, my spirit is envious and frets at the wealth and success of secular men. I know I shouldn't, for they will soon wither and die away like green grass. Help me not to fret when men succeed in their wicked schemes. Teach me to be still before you, and wait patiently for you. In a little while you will cut off evil men and they will be no more. You laugh at the wicked for you know their day of judgment is coming. They will vanish like smoke. Though a ruthless man flourish like a green tree in its native soil, he will soon pass away. All sinners will be destroyed and cut off from your blessings.

Teach me, Lord, to trust in you and to do good, fully realizing that I am enjoying a safe pasture. You have promised me, "Delight yourself in me, your Lord, and I will give you the desires of your heart." O my soul, commit your way to the Lord. Trust in him, then he will make your goodness shine like the dawn and the justice of your cause like the noonday sun. I will stop fretting at men's success and be still before you, Lord. I will wait patiently for your provision, until I inherit the land and enjoy great peace.

In times of disaster I will not wither; in days of famine I will enjoy plenty, because you know and order my future days. You love the just and protect them. You will never forsake your faithful ones. You make their steps firm. Though they stumble, they will not fall since you hold their hand. It is so much better to have little according to your will, than to gain wealth against your will.

Yes, I will wait for the Lord and keep his way. In his time he will exalt me to inherit the land and I will see the wicked cut off. Lord, you are my stronghold in troubled times; rescue comes only from you. I will wait for your deliverance and provision with a spirit full of contentment and peace. Give me the faith and patience I need. Bless me with more contentment. May I be able to honestly say with Paul in Philippians 4:12-13, "I know what it is to be in need, and I know what it is to have plenty. I have learned the secret of being content in any and every situation, whether well fed or hungry, whether living in plenty or in want. I can do everything through him who gives me strength."

(Psalm 37)

You warn me not to be overawed when a man grows rich and the splendor of his wealth increases, for he will take nothing with him when he dies. He will not take his wealth with him to the grave.

(Psalm 49:16-17)

It is true that whoever loves money never has money enough, and whoever loves wealth is never satisfied with his income. Help me to be perfectly content with whatever my income is.

(Ecclesiastes 5:10)

Praying for Direction

"I am the Lord your God, who teaches you what is best for you, who directs you in the way you should go. If only you had paid attention to my commands, your peace would have been like a river, your righteousness like the waves of the sea."

(Isaiah 48:17-18)

Praying for Fear of the Lord

You have said, "for I, the Lord your God, am a jealous God, punishing the children for the sin of the fathers to the third and fourth generation of those who hate me."

(Deut. 5:9)

Praying for Generosity

You have asked me, Lord, to be openhanded toward my needy brothers and toward the poor and needy in the land. You said, "give generously and do so without a grudging heart; then because of this you would bless me in all my work and in everything I put my hand to.

(Deut. 15:10-11)

Praying for God's Help

At your mere word, the sky with all its stars and galaxies came into being. At your mere word, the earth was formed with all its oceans and rivers, mountains and plains, with all its thousands of types of animals and birds and fish, all its trees and flowers. O Lord, look upon my situation and speak your creative word that will bring victory. Use your almighty power to have mercy on me, your child and servant. Create your perfect solution to my problems.

Gen. 1)

Jesus, my Lord and savior, fight against those who fight against me. Take up your shield and hasten to help me. Draw your spear and wave your battle-axe against those who pursue and persecute me. Assure my heart, "I am your salvation, your deliverance. I will rescue you."

(Psalm 35)

Praying for Grace to Forgive Others

O Lord, I have been sinned against, and I am so angry, so full of rage. I want them punished. I want them to pay for all the misery they have caused me. I know you want me to forgive and forget, but I don't have the power in me. You will have to give me the grace to forgive them and love them. O Lord, my father, give me the spirit of Joseph. He was sold into slavery by his brothers, falsely accused and thrown into prison. He was in slavery and prison all unjustly, for many years. Yet he continued to love and serve you. He didn't blame you. He forgave and loved his brothers who started his many years of being mistreated. Lord, give me the spirit of Joseph. Help me to forgive, forget, and to love those who have mistreated me. Deliver me from the prison of hatred and lack of forgiveness. Deliver me from the cancer of bitterness. Give me joy and a lighthearted spirit, so that I can love everyone and laugh at the future, because you are in control of all the circumstances of my life, and you have great and wonderful things planned for me.

(Genesis 50:15-21)

Praying for the Holy Spirit

You have promised, Lord, that when the Holy Spirit is poured upon us from on high, the desert will become a fertile field, and the fertile field will seem like a forest. Justice and righteousness will reign. The fruit of righteousness will be peace and the effect of righteousness will be quietness and confidence forever. Your people will live in secure homes, in undisturbed places of rest. They will be blessed even though hail flattens the forest and the city is leveled completely. O Lord, I want your Holy Spirit to be poured upon my life. I want him to dwell richly within me so I may live in righteousness and enjoy the safety and peace it brings regardless of the circumstances of life. I want to be so secure in you, that I fear nothing in the present or the future. By your Spirit may I rest secure in your provision.

(Isaiah 32:15-20)

Praying for Hope, Renewal

O Lord, give me the confidence that with your help, my future can be free from the failures of my past. You said, "Forget the former things; do not dwell on the past. See, I am doing a new thing." Lord, release me from my past and do a new thing in my life.

(Isaiah 43:18)

You have promised your Spirit, whom I so desperately need, when you said, "I will pour water on the thirsty land, and streams on the dry ground; I will pour out my Spirit on your offerings, and my blessing on your descendants." Lord, I am a thirsty land. Please pour out your Spirit on me.

(Isaiah 44:3)

Praying for Joy

I groan and sigh, O King, and cry to you for help. You are my Lord and God. Who else should I cry to? Who else has your loving-kindness? Who else has your almighty power? In the morning when I lay my requests before you, you hear them. I wait and eagerly watch for your mercy. I bow down reverently before you in my quiet place of prayer, as I worship you in church. Lead me, O Lord, to do what is right according to your will. Make my path straight and level. Make your will for the next steps of my life obvious and easy. Lord, spread your protection over me. Let me and all who take refuge in you be glad and always sing a cheerful tune. For surely, O Lord, you bless your servants who do right, and build a wall of protection around them. Give me a joyous spirit as I serve you.

(Psalm 5)

You have said I should rejoice before you in everything I put my hand to. Help me to have a joyful spirit in every task.

(Deut. 12:18)

Fill my heart with joy, O Lord, so that I will feel like shouting, "Shout for joy, O heavens, and rejoice, O earth! Burst into song, O mountains! For the Lord comforts his people and will have compassion on his afflicted ones." You have assured me of your care for me when you said, "Can a mother forget the baby at her breasts and have no compassion on the child she birthed? Though she may forget, I will not forget you! See, I have engraved you on the palms of my hands."

(Isaiah 49:13-16)

Praying for Light and Joy

O Lord, you have made promises in your Word. Fulfill these promises in my life for I need your touch. You've promised many things: people walking in darkness have seen a great light; a light has dawned on those living in the shadow of death; you have increased their joy with the joy of harvest time; you have shattered the yoke that burdens them and lifted the bar across their shoulders. You have done this through your son Jesus, born to us a child, called Wonderful, Counselor, Mighty God, Everlasting Father and Prince of Peace. O Lord, may Jesus' government of my life increase without end. Send Jesus to be my light, teaching me how to live and to be my counselor, helping me to make all the decisions of my life. O Jesus, bring me peace as I yield to your guidance, especially when I walk in darkness and in the shadow of death. Do something wonderful in my life. Be my counselor, my joy, and my prince of peace.

(Isaiah 9:2-7)

Praying for an Obedient Spirit

Help me, O Lord, to be obedient to you in every aspect of my life. You have warned me, "Woe to him who quarrels with his Maker, to him who is but a potsherd among the potsherds on the ground. Does the clay say to the potter, 'What are you making?'" Rid me of any such rebellious attitudes. Give me a heart eager to do your will.

(Isaiah 45:9)

Praying for Peace

Lord, you have promised to keep in perfect peace him whose mind is steadfast and who trusts in you. You make the way of the righteous smooth, his path level. My soul yearns for you in the night and in the morning my spirit longs for you. Lord, help me to wait for you as I walk according to your scriptures. May your name and fame be the greatest desire of my heart. O my soul, trust in the Lord forever, for he is the Lord, the Rock eternal.

(Isaiah 26:3-12)

Praying for Perspective

Show me, O Lord, my life from the perspective of its end. Let me know how fleeting and frail my life is. You have made my days the mere width of a hand, a mere breath. My span of years is as nothing before you. I am a mere ghost bustling back and forth mostly in vain, heaping up wealth, not knowing who will get it. Help me avoid making my life a vain show, busy doing things that matter not for eternity. Help me focus my priorities on things important for all eternity.

(Psalm 39:4-6)

May I recognize the emptiness of temporal things. All men are like grass and all their glory is like the flowers of the field. The grass withers and the flowers fall oh so quickly. People, with all their opinions and endeavors, disappear as quickly as the grass withers and the flowers fall. But your truths in the Bible stand forever.

(Isaiah 40:6-8)

Praying for Protection

I call upon you confidently, O God, because you hear my prayers and answer my requests. Show me again the wonder of your great love, how those who take refuge in you are always saved from their foes by your almighty hand. Keep me as the apple of your eye, and hide me from my enemies in the shadow of your wings. Rise up, O Lord, confront and bring down my enemies. Save me from men of this world, whose only reward is in this life.

(Psalm 17:6-9, 13, 14)

Hear my cry, O God. From the ends of the earth I call to you as my heart grows faint. Please lead me to the rock that is higher than I. For you have been my strong tower of refuge against the foe. O how I long to dwell in your tent forever and take refuge in the shelter of your wings.

(Psalm 61:1-4)

Hear my complaint, O God. Protect my life from the threat of the enemy. Hide me from the conspiracy of the wicked. They sharpen their tongues like swords and aim their words like deadly arrows. Without fear they suddenly shoot from ambush at the innocent.

(Psalm 64:1-4)

Praying for Revival

O Shepherd of your people, you who sits enthroned between the cherubim, hear our prayer. Awaken your might and come to save us. Make your face shine upon us that we may be rescued. Restore us, O Lord God Almighty. How long will your anger smolder against the prayers of your people? Our enemies mock us; you have made us drink tears by the bowlful. Look upon us and save us from our enemies. Send with power your son and our Lord Jesus Christ. Then we will not turn away from you. Revive us and we will call upon your name. Surround us with your presence and revive your church.

(Psalm 80)

You have given an answer to our prayer. You've said, "Hear, O my people, and I will warn you, if you would but listen to me. In your distress you called and I rescued you. I removed the burden of sin from your shoulders. I am the Lord your God who saved you from the slavery of sin. Open wide your mouth and I will fill it. But my people would not listen to me and obey me. So I gave them over to their stubborn hearts to follow their own devices. But if my people would only listen to me, if my church would just follow my ways, how quickly would I subdue their enemies and turn my hand against their foes, who would cringe before me! You would be fed with the finest of wheat. With honey from the rock I would satisfy you."

(Psalm 81)

In the past, O Lord, you forgave all our sins. You set aside all your fierce anger. Restore us again, O God our Savior, and put away your displeasure toward us. Will you be angry with us forever? Will you prolong your anger through all generations? Will you not revive us again, so that your people may rejoice in you? Show us your mercy and unfailing love, O Lord, and grant us your salvation.

You have promised peace to your saints, but they shouldn't return to folly. Surely your salvation is near those who fear you, so that your glory may dwell on the earth. Love, faithfulness, peace, and righteousness all prepare the way for your working in our presence. Revive us, O Lord, change our hearts and lives so that you can come and have your way with us. You will indeed give what is good, and your harvest will be great.

(Psalm 85)

Praying for Salvation of the World

Arise, O God, who rides on the clouds, and scatter your enemies. Make your foes flee before you, as smoke is blown away by the wind and as wax melts before fire. Make your church rejoice and be glad before you as your kingdom triumphs throughout the world.

(Psalm 68:1-4)

O Lord Jesus, king of the universe, come quickly. Come to judge your people in righteousness and your afflicted ones with justice. When you come you will defend the afflicted and save the children of the needy. You will crush the oppressor. Your kingdom will endure through all generations. You will be like rain watering the earth. Prosperity will abound with righteous. You will rule the entire world. Nations will bring gifts and bow before you. Your enemies will lick the dust. All nations will serve you. You will deliver the needy who cry out with no one to help. You will rescue victims of oppression and violence, for they are precious in your sight. May your name be blessed forever because all nations will be blessed through you. They will all call you blessed. Praise be to you, O Lord God, who alone does marvelous deeds. May the whole earth be filled with your glory.

(Psalm 72)

O God, be gracious to your church and make your face shine upon us, so that your ways may be known on earth and your salvation known among all the nations. May all the nations learn to praise you and be glad, and sing to you because you rule all peoples justly, and guide all the governments of the earth. You will bless us, Lord, and all the ends of the earth will fear you. Do it soon, Lord, soon.

(Psalm 67)

O Lord Jesus, it was prophesied that you would come and judge the needy with righteousness, and give just decisions for the poor of the earth. Come quickly, Lord Jesus. Strike the earth with the rod of your mouth. Slay the wicked with your breath. Make the earth full of the knowledge of the Lord as the waters cover the sea. O Lord, come quickly to rescue the peoples of every language and nation.

(Isaiah 11:3-9)

Praying for Strength

The words of David to Solomon apply to me: "Be strong and courageous, and do the work. Do not be afraid or discouraged, for the Lord God is with you. He will not fail you or forsake you until all your work in his service is finished." Lord, help me to be strong and courageous because of your strength and faithfulness.

(1 Chronicles 29:20)

Praying for Unsaved Friend

My heart is heavy, O Lord, because my friend has not been saved and born again into your family. Please strengthen his feeble hands and steady his wobbling knees. Say to his fearful heart, "Be strong, do not fear; your God will come to save you." May his blind eyes be opened and his deaf ears unstopped. May his lame legs leap like a deer and his mute tongue shout for you.

He is an unclean and wicked fool who has been avoiding the highway called the Way of Holiness. He has refused to walk in that Way. O Lord, change his heart and reveal yourself to him so he will join the redeemed and walk with them on this Way of Holiness. May he enter Zion with singing and may everlasting joy crown his head. May gladness and joy overtake him and sorrow and sighing flee away. Come Lord, and grant him eternal life, I pray.

(Isaiah 35:3-10)

Praying for Wisdom

O Lord, help me to follow your instruction, "Do not add to what I command you and do not subtract from it, but keep the commands of the Lord your God." (Deut. 4:2). This is my heart's desire. As I hear various winds of doctrine, help me to clearly understand the truth and not to add or subtract from your word. Teach me how to be careful and firmly make sure I do not forget your word, nor let the truths of the Bible slip from my heart as long as I live.

(Deut. 4:9)

Praying for World Peace

O Lord Jesus, it was prophesied that the oppressor will come to an end, that destruction will cease and the aggressor will vanish from the land. And that a throne will be established in love for you, and you will sit on it in faithfulness, judging justly and speeding the cause of righteousness. O Lord, come quickly and deliver the world from all its wretchedness.

(Isaiah 16:4-5)

Come, Lord Jesus, and judge the nations and settle their disputes. Let your law govern all the nations of the world, so that they will beat their swords into plowshares and their spears into pruning hooks, so that nation will not take up sword against nation and so nations will not train for war anymore. Give us world peace, O Lord, and protect us from all the ravages of war.

(Isaiah 2:3-4)

God Controls All

The heavens praise your wonders, O Lord. For who among the heavenly beings can compare with you. You are more awesome than all the angels who surround you. O Lord God, you are all powerful. All the earth and the skies are yours, for you founded the world and all that is in it. You created the north and the south. You rule over the surging sea. Righteousness and justice are the foundation of your throne; love and faithfulness go before you. Blessed are those who have learned to praise you and walk in the light of your presence. They rejoice at the thought of you all day long and rejoice in your righteousness. For you are their glory and strength, and by your favor do we prosper. You alone are our king.

(Psalm 89:5-18)

No country is saved by the size of its army. No soldier escapes by his great strength. Neither are advanced weapons a guarantee of victory.

(Psalm 33:16-17)

Let all the nations shout to God with cries of joy for he is the great King over all the earth. He is the Lord Most High, causing great awe and terrifying dread. He subdues nations and gives us the land he picks for our inheritance. Let us sing praises to our God, who sits on his holy throne and reigns over all the nations. He is greatly exalted over all the powers of this world, because all the kings of the earth belong to him.

(Psalm 47)

You rule forever by your power. Since your eyes watch the nations, may no one rebel against you.

(Psalm 66:7)

The Lord Almighty has sworn, "Surely, as I have planed, so it will be, and as I have purposed, so it will stand." For the Lord Almighty has purposed, and who can thwart him? His hand is stretched out, and who can turn it back?

(Isaiah 14:24,27)

O Almighty God, you control all things. You control not only the forces of nature, but also all the affairs of kings and nations—even godless ones. You talked about Cyrus 170 years before he was born: "He is my shepherd and he will accomplish all that I please. He will say of Jerusalem, 'Let it be rebuilt.'" You said you would take hold of his right hand to subdue nations before him and to strip kings of their armor, to open doors before him so that gates will not be shut. "I will cut down gates of bronze and cut through bars of iron. I will give you riches stored in secret places. I call you by name and bestow on you a title of honor, though you do not acknowledge me. I am the Lord, and there is no other; apart from me there is no God. I will strengthen you, though you have not acknowledged me, so that from sunrise to sunset men may know there is none besides me. I am the Lord, and there is no other. I form the light and create darkness. I bring prosperity and create disaster; I, the Lord, do all these things." If you so control the affairs of godless men, how much more will you control the circumstances of my life since I am your servant and even your child.

(Isaiah 45:1-7)

God Gives Abundant Life

O Lord, how precious is your unfailing love! Men, both high and low, find refuge in the shadow of your wings. They feast on the abundance of your house. You give them drink from your river of delights, for with you is the fountain of life, and by your light we see clearly and truly.

(Psalm 36:7-9)

I waited patiently for you, Lord, and you heard my cry. You lifted me out of the slimy pit full of muck and mire, and set my feet on a rock, so I would have a firm place to stand. You put a new song in my heart, a hymn of praise to my God. Certainly the man is blessed who puts his trust in you, who does not follow those who are proud, or pursue false and empty hopes. O Lord my God, so many are the wonders you have done for me that I cannot possibly count or declare them. Here I am, Lord, from deep within my heart I declare that your wish is my command, for my greatest desire is to do your will.

(Psalm 40:1-8)

God Gives Salvation

O Lord, we sing to you a new song, for you have done marvelous things. Your right hand and holy arm have worked salvation for us. You have made your salvation known and revealed your righteousness to the nations. You have been faithful and loving to your people and all the ends of the earth have seen the salvation of our God. May all the earth shout for joy to you, Lord. May they burst into jubilant song and make music to you, O King, with trumpets and strings and singing. Let the sea roar and everything in it. Let the world resound and all who live in it. Let the rivers clap their hands and the mountains sing together for joy. Let them all sing before you, Lord, for you are coming to judge the earth with righteousness.

My soul finds rest in you alone, O God, for my salvation comes from you. I will never be shaken because you alone are the rock of my salvation. Find rest, O my soul, in God alone, since all hope comes from him; all salvation and honor depend on him. He is my mighty fortress. Trust in him at all times. Pour out your heart to him when troubled. Do not set your heart on riches or trust in wealth.

Put all your trust in God who alone gives salvation.

(Psalm 62:1-10)

I praise you, O God, for you daily bear my burdens. You are the sovereign Lord who saves and provides escape from death. You are awesome in your sanctuary, the God who gives power and strength to his people. May your praises always be on my lips.

(Psalm 68:19-20,35)

God Is Almighty

O Lord, may the earth rejoice because you reign on your throne with righteousness and justice. You are surrounded with clouds and darkness. Fire goes before you consuming foes on every side. The earth sees your lightning and trembles. The mountains melt like wax before you, O God, for you are Lord over all the earth. All the peoples of the world see your glory. Your people rejoice because of your judgments, O Lord, for you are the Most High over all the earth, far exalted above all gods. We rejoice in you, Lord, and praise your holy name, because you guard the lives of your faithful ones and deliver them from the hand of the wicked. You fill your saints full of light and joy. Praise your name.

(Psalm 97)

O Lord, there is no one like you in holiness or power. You reign supreme over all, hence I don't fear my enemies since you are my deliverer. You have complete power over all the circumstances of my life. You break the bows of warriors, but those who stumble are armed with strength. Those who had plenty to eat end up on welfare, but those who were hungry no longer hunger. She who had many children pines away in loneliness, but she who was barren is blessed with many children. You are in complete control, Lord. You bring death or make alive, you send poverty or wealth, you humble or exalt. You raise the poor from the dust so that they inherit a throne. You guard the feet of your saints, while the wicked lose their way in darkness. It is not by human strength that anyone prevails, for anyone who opposes you Lord will be shattered when you judge the ends of the earth. But you give power to your anointed. O Lord, my heart rejoices in you.

(1 Samuel 2:1-10)

"No one can deliver out of my hand. When I act, who can reverse it?"

(Isaiah 43:13)

"I am God, and there is none like me. I make known the end from the beginning, from ancient times I have made known what is still to come. I say: 'My purpose will stand, and I will do all that I please.' What I have said, that will I bring about; what I have planned, that will I do."

(Isaiah 46:9-11)

God Is Our Creator

We come before you, O Lord, to sing for joy and extol you with music and songs to express our thanksgiving. For you are the great God, the great King above all gods. In your hands are the depths of the earth. The mountain peaks belong to you. The sea is yours, for you made it, and your hands formed the dry land. We bow down and worship you on our knees, O Lord our Maker, for you are our God and we are the flock under your care in your pasture.

(Psalm 95:1-7)

God Knows All

Does he who implanted the ear not hear? Does he who formed the eye not see? Does he who teaches man lack knowledge? The Lord knows the thoughts of man. He knows that they are futile.

(Psalm 94:9-11)

You look down from heaven, Lord, and see all mankind. You watch all who live on earth. You carefully consider everything your creatures do.

(Psalm 33:13-15)

God Protects His Children

O Lord, you are my refuge and my fortress. You are my God in whom I trust, because you have promised me that he who dwells in the shelter of the Most High will rest in the shadow of the Almighty. You have promised to save me from traps and plagues, that you would cover me with your feathers so that under your wings I will find safety. Your faithfulness will be my shield and protection against the enemy. I will not fear the terror of night, nor arrows, nor plagues. Though people fall all around me, I will not be struck down. I will be an untouched spectator of the destruction around me. You have promised that if I make you, the Most High, my dwelling and my refuge, then no harm will befall me, no disaster will come near my home. For you will command your angels to guard me in all my ways. They will lift me up in their hands so that I will not strike my foot against a stone. I will tread upon the lion and trample the serpent without being hurt. O Lord my God, you spoke these words to me: "Because you love me, I will rescue you. I will protect you since you acknowledge my name. When you call upon me I will answer you. I will be with you in trouble. I will deliver you and honor you. With long life

I will satisfy you and show you my salvation." Praise the Lord, for God is so good

(Psalm 91)

God's Presence Is Good

How lovely is your dwelling place, O Lord Almighty! My soul yearns, even faints, for your courts. My heart and flesh cry out for the living God, O Lord Almighty, my King and my God. Blessed are those who dwell in your house constantly praising you. Blessed are those whose strength is in you and who have set their hearts on seeking your presence. Even as they pass through a dry place, they make it a place of springs and rain filled pools. They go from strength to strength till each appears in your presence. Hear my prayer, O Lord, and look with favor upon me. Better is one day in your courts than a thousand elsewhere. I would rather be in your house than anywhere else on earth. For you bestow favor and honor and do not withhold any good thing from those whose walk is blameless. O Lord Almighty, blessed is the man who trusts in you.

(Psalm 84)

God Provides Money

O Lord, let me never say to myself, "My power and the strength of my hands have produced this wealth for me." But let me always remember that it is you, Lord, who gives me the ability to produce wealth, and so confirm your promises to me.

(Deut. 8:17-18)

You have promised that if I faithfully obey your commands—to love you and serve you with all my heart and with all my soul—that you would send rain on my land in its season, both autumn and spring rains, so that I may gather in my grain, new wine and oil, and that you will provide grass in the fields for my cattle, and I will eat and be satisfied.

(Deut. 11:13-15)

God's Word Is Good For Me

Your Bible, O God, is perfect instruction, reviving my soul. Your teachings are trustworthy, making even the simple wise. Your commands are right, giving joy to my heart and light to my eyes. Your Word is sweeter than honey and more precious than tons of gold. When I meditate on its truths, awe, respect, and fear of you, O Lord God Almighty, fill my soul. May the words of my mouth, O Lord, and the meditation of my heart be pleasing in your sight.

Your law warns me; living by it brings great reward. Lord, I do not know all my faults. Please forgive my hidden faults. I am your servant and want to always do your will, but sometimes I fail. Keep me also from my willful sins; may they not rule over me. Only then will I be blameless and innocent of great transgression. May I do all things for your honor and glory, O Lord, my strength and my redeemer.

(Psalm 19:7-14)

Your word, O Lord, is always right, always true. You are faithful and true in all you do.

(Psalm 33:40)

The Grandeur of God

O Lord, you alone are the source of all wisdom and power. There is none like you. Who has measured how many handfuls of water there is in the seas, or has measured how many hand widths there are between the stars? Who has held the dust of the earth in a basket or weighed the mountains? Only you, Lord. Who instructed you and served as your counselor? Whom did you go to for consultation on the right way to do things? Who was your teacher? Surely the wisdom and power of the nations are like a drop in a bucket and like dust on a scale. Before you all the nations are as nothing. They are worthless, less than nothing. Is there anyone you can be compared with? No. Not a single one. You are unique. You sit enthroned above the universe. People are like grasshoppers and you reduce their rulers to nothing. No sooner are they planted, no sooner sown, no sooner do they take root, than you blow on them and they wither, and a whirlwind sweeps them away like chaff. Lord, you have no equal. There is not even one who remotely compares to you. You alone created the universe with power and wisdom that no one can fathom.

(Isaiah 40:12-26)

The Lord Alone Is God

Lord, you declare your sovereignty so clearly. "I am the first and I am the last; apart from me there is no God. Who is like me? Let him prove it by foretelling the future. Is there any God besides me? No, there is no other Rock; not a single one."

(Isaiah 6-8)

The Lord Alone Will Be Worshiped

You have declared from on high: "Turn to me and be saved, all you ends of the earth; for I am God, and there is no other. By myself I have sworn, my mouth has uttered in all integrity a word that will not be revoked: Before me every knee will bow; by me every tongue will swear. They will say of me, 'In the Lord alone are righteousness and strength.'" All who have raged against you will eventually come to you and be put to shame. Lord, may I worship you now and give you all the honor that you deserve. May I serve you faithfully now so that when I come into your presence, I will not be put to shame.

(Isaiah 45:22-24)

The Lord Is My Strength

I love you, Lord Jesus. You are my shield, my rock, my fortress, my rescuer, and my strength. In the stronghold of your protection I take refuge. When I call on you, I am saved from my enemies. Who is like you Lord? Your right hand sustains me; you stoop down to make me great. You arm me with strength and make my way perfect. You make my feet like the feet of a mountain deer, enabling me to stand on the treacherous heights without slipping. You set me securely upon my high places. You clear and level the path before me, so that I won't stumble or sprain my ankle. You train my hands for battle and make my aim perfect. Your instruction is flawless. With your help I can scale a wall and advance against a troop. O Lord, you are indeed my strength and my sure victory.

(Psalm 18:1-3,28-36)

There is no one like you, O Lord, who rides on the clouds in your majesty to help your people. You are our refuge forever, and underneath are your everlasting arms. You will drive out our enemies before us, so that we will live in safety, secure in a land of grain and new wine. How blessed are we, because you are our shield and glorious sword, making our enemies cower.

(Deut. 33:26-29)

And as I promised to Moses, so I promise you, "I'll never leave you or forsake you. Therefore, be strong and courageous. Do not be terrified; do not be discouraged, for the Lord your God will be with you wherever you go."

(Joshua 1:5-9)

The Lord Provides All My Needs

You are my shepherd, O Lord. I shall never need anything. You make me lie down in fresh green pastures, and lead me beside still and peaceful waters. You refresh my soul. You guide me in paths of holiness so that my life brings honor to your name. Even though I face death, I will fear no evil, for you are with me. Your rod of protection and your staff of guidance comfort me. Even in the presence of my enemies, you prepare a banquet table for me. You anoint my head with oil, and fill my cup to overflowing. Surely your goodness, unfailing love, and mercy will follow me all the days of my life, and I will dwell in the house of the Lord my God forever. How wonderful is my God! How wonderful and secure is my future!

(Psalm 23)

May I taste and see how good your are, Lord, how blessed I will be when I take refuge in you. May all your saints fear you, for those who fear you lack nothing. The lions may grow weak and hungry, but those who seek you, Lord, lack no good thing.

(Psalm 34:8-10)

The Lord Rescues His Children

Now I know that the Lord saves his children. He answers their prayers from his holy heaven with the rescuing power of his strong arm. Some trust in guns and airplanes, some in bombs and missiles, but we trust in the name of the Lord our God. They fall, but we rise up and stand firm. O Lord, save your children! Answer us when we call.

(Psalm 20)

You, O Lord, have risen up for me against the wicked. Unless you had given me help, I would have been put to death. But when I said, "My foot is slipping," your love supported me. When anxiety was great within me, your consolation brought joy to my soul.

(Psalm 94:16-19)

My soul will rejoice in you, My Lord, and delight in your salvation. My whole being will exclaim, "Who is like you, O Lord? You rescue the poor and the afflicted from those too strong for them, and the needy from those who rob and exploit them.

(Psalm 35:9-10)

Lord, you watch over your children, those who are confidently expecting your unfailing love. You deliver them from death and keep them alive in famine. We are waiting for you, Lord, confident that you are our help and protection. Our hearts rejoice because we can trust in your faithfulness. May your unfailing love rest upon us as we patiently wait for your deliverance.

(Psalm 33:18-22)

Lord, you hear your saints when they cry out to you and deliver them from all their distress and troubles. You are close to the brokenhearted and rescue the depressed, those crushed in spirit and humbly repentant. Many are the troubles and afflictions of a holy man, but you deliver him out of them all.

(Psalm 34:17-19)

Salvation Will Be Victorious

"Listen to me, my people. The law will go out from me and my justice will become a light to the nations. My righteousness draws near speedily. My salvation is on the way. My arm will bring justice to the nations. The islands will look to me and wait in hope for my arm. Lift up your eyes to the heavens. They will vanish like smoke. Look at the earth below. It will wear out like a garment and its inhabitants die like flies. But my salvation will last forever. My righteousness will never fail. Hear me my people who have my law in your hearts. Do not fear the reproach of men or be terrified by their insults, for worms will devour them, but my righteousness and salvation will last through all generations." O Lord, we look forward eagerly to the time when the redeemed will enter Zion with singing, when everlasting joy will crown our heads, when gladness and joy will overtake us and sorrow and sighing will flee away.

(Isaiah 51:4-8, 11)

Specialized Prayers

Of a Farmer

When the heavens are shut up and there is no rain because we your people have sinned against you, and when we pray and confess your name and turn from our sins, then hear from heaven and forgive us our sins. Teach us the right way to live, and send rain on the land that you have given us. When any disaster may strike—famine, blight, mildew, locust, hail—and when we pray to you, each one aware of the afflictions of his own heart, then hear from heaven. Forgive and act. Deal with each one of us according to all he does since you know our hearts, so that we may fear and serve you all of our days.

1 Kings 8: 35-40)

Of a Healed Person

In my sickness I said, "In the prime of my life must I go through the gates of death and be robbed of the rest of my years? No longer will I look on mankind, or be with my loved ones who now dwell in this world. Like a tent my house has been pulled down and taken from me. Like a rug my life has been rolled up and cut off from the loom. I eagerly looked for a dawn to my night of suffering. I moaned like a mourning dove. My eyes grew weak as I looked to the heavens. I cried out, 'O Lord, come to my aid!' But God broke all my bones and was making an end of me."

But now what can I say to you, my Lord and Savior? You answered my prayer and healed me! You restored me to health and let me live. Surely it was for my benefit that I suffered such anguish. In your love you kept me from the pit of destruction. You have put all my sins behind your back. Surely I will walk humbly all my years and praise you as I am doing today. I will tell my children of your faithfulness. I will sing your praises in your temple all the days of my life.

(Isaiah 38:10-2)

Of a Missionary

Your call to me, Lord, is like your call to Abraham. You are asking me to leave my country, my people, and my parents and relatives, to go to a land you have chosen for me. And part of your promise to Abraham applies to me. You will bless me and cause me to be a blessing to others. You will bless those who help me and curse those who oppose me, and peoples on this earth will be blessed through me. How awesome is your call! What a privilege to be commissioned in your service. Generation after generation will be blessed by you through me, even long after my work is done. How wonderful! How awesome! How terrifying!

(Gen. 12:1-3)

Like Isaiah I am thinking, "Woe is me. I am ruined. For I am unclean. I am a weak sinner who cannot perform this awesome work." But with a burning coal you took away Isaiah's sins. O Lord, by the blood of Jesus, change my sins to be as white as snow. Make me worthy of your trust. Empower me to do your work faithfully, so in the end I will hear you say, "Well done, thou good and faithful servant." You ask, Lord, "Whom shall I send? Who will go for us?" I respond, "Here am I. Send me!"

(Isaiah 6:5-8)

Does your promise to Jacob apply to me, Lord? You told him, "I am the Lord your God. I am with you and will watch over you wherever you go, and I will bring you back to this land. I will not leave you until I have done what I have promised you." (Genesis 28:15) Since I go on my mission sent by you, I know you will watch over me as you did Jacob. I know you will be with me wherever I go, and stay with me until your work through me is completed.

Of a Preacher

Lord, may I always follow your instructions. You have told us who preach your gospel to shout it from the mountain tops, to lift up our voices with a shout and not be afraid to go to all the cities and proclaim "here is your God!"

(Isaiah 40:9)

Of a Retired Person

It is good to praise you, Lord, and make music to your name, O Most High, to proclaim your love in the morning and your faithfulness at night. For you make me glad by your deeds. I sing for joy at the works of your hands. How great are your works and how profound your thoughts! You have exalted my strength like that of a wild ox. My eyes have seen the defeat of my adversaries. I've seen what you have declared, that the righteous will flourish like a palm tree. Planted in the house of the Lord, they will grow like a cedar of Lebanon. They will still bear fruit in old age. They will stay fresh and green, proclaiming, "The Lord is upright. He is my rock and there is no wickedness in him.

(Psalm 92)

Thank you, Lord, for your faithful care, as you have said, "Even to your old age and gray hairs I am he, I am he who will sustain you; I will sustain you and I will rescue you.

(Isaiah 46:4)

Of a Servant of the Lord

O Lord, you are my God and I am your servant. Guard my life for I am devoted to you and trust you. Have mercy on me for I am poor and needy and call to you all day long. Bring joy to your servant for I lift up my soul to you. You are forgiving and good, O Lord, abounding in love to all who call to you. You are a compassionate and gracious God, slow to anger and abounding in love and faithfulness. Please hear my prayer. I know you will answer me when I call to you when I am having a difficult time.

There are no gods like you. You alone have done wonderful deeds. Eventually all the nations you have made will come and worship before you. I will greatly rejoice when I see you so glorified. For you are great and you alone are God.

Teach me your ways, O God, and I will walk in your truth. Give me an undivided heart that I may fear and honor your name. I will glorify your name forever with all my heart, for great is your love toward me. Turn to me and have mercy on me. Give your strength to your servant. Give me a sign of your goodness so that my enemies may see it and be put to shame.

Lord, you are always my comfort and my help. I thank you and rejoice in being your servant, for you are such a gracious master.

(Psalm 86)

Lord, before I was born you called me. You made my mouth like a sharpened sword and you hid me in the shadow of your hand. You made me into a polished arrow and concealed me in your quiver. You said to me, "you are my servant in whom I will display my splendor." Though I sometimes feel I have labored to no purpose and have spent my strength for nothing, I know that what is due me is in my Lord's hand and my reward is with my God."

(Isaiah 49:1-5)

CPSIA information can be obtained at www.ICGtesting.com
Printed in the USA
LVOW030347201011

251265LV00001B/2/P